How to Win an Election

An Essential Guide to Campaigning During Adversity

By Kurt Thigpen

"It is not the critic who counts; not the man who points out how the strong man stumbles, or where the doer of deeds could have done them better. The credit belongs to the man who is actually in the arena, whose face is marred by dust and sweat and blood; who strives valiantly; who errs, who comes short again and again, because there is no effort without error and shortcoming; but who does actually strive to do the deeds; who knows great enthusiasms, the great devotions; who spends himself in a worthy cause; who at the best knows, in the end, the triumph of high achievement, and who at the worst, if he fails, at least fails while daring greatly, so that his place shall never be with those cold and timid souls who neither know victory nor defeat."

- **Theodore Roosevelt**

How to Win an Election
An Essential Guide to Campaigning During Adversity
By Kurt Thigpen
Cover design by Martin Rodriguez
Edited by Cameya Martin
Printed in the United States of America

Dedication

I'd like to thank my former campaign manager, Adam Czajkowski of Tallac Strategies, for encouraging me, guiding me, pushing me outside of my comfort zone, and helping me realize a dream I never thought possible.

To my best friend, and PR badass, Rachel Gattuso of the Gattuso Coalition, thank you for helping to ensure I always stayed calm, prepared, poised, and ready to go for any speech or media interview.

And to my husband, Chris Thigpen, thank you for believing in me and supporting me through the campaign, and for helping me through everything that happened after. You are my rock and I couldn't have started this journey without you.

Before We Go On, Here's My Story

Since I was very young, I remember wanting to be involved in my community; from Boy Scouts, to 4-H club, to student leadership in high school. I enjoyed it, as it gave me purpose and helped me grow as a person. Not to toot my own horn, but I learned I was very good at being a team player, making a compelling argument, and governing in general. I dreamt of maybe one day pursuing a career in public service, but the politics of it all scared me, and I also didn't think my background would make me "electable".

I don't come from family money, am openly gay (member since 2004), and wasn't born and raised in Nevada (which always felt like a requirement to run for office here with those touting 5th generation status), even though I've lived here for over 10 years after moving here from Georgia.

It wasn't until I saw Mayor Pete Buttigieg (now U.S. Secretary of Transportation) enter the national stage in his run for the presidency, with his husband and two dogs in tow, did I feel it was possible for someone like me to run for office. Regardless of your political leanings, his run was deeply inspiring and historic.

Shortly after, my soon-to-be campaign manager, Adam Czajkowski, reached out to me about an open seat on the Washoe County School Board after he read some of my local writings about various community concerns related to school safety.

From there, as they say, the rest is history!

My campaign launched in January 2020 and by March, everything changed. Just days after I filed my official candidate paperwork, Nevada joined most of the country in going into lockdown mode, throwing me and my campaign team for a loop as to what to do ahead of the June primary election.

I remember the talking points back then being "this will blow over in a couple of weeks, let's pause for now," and as of writing this book, the pandemic hasn't ended.

So, my campaign had to pivot, like many others.

Luckily, my 10+ years of experience in digital marketing & branding (I own a small marketing agency) became my secret weapon. I felt like the election was in my territory now, which was a little exciting to see play out.

From March, leading up to the June 2020 primary, my campaign manager and I brainstormed alternatives to traditional field campaign strategies. I would convert the traditional methods into strategic communication and advertising strategies that would safely and effectively reach the specific voters that lived in the school district area I lived in.

On June 9, 2020, I was honored to be elected as a trustee on the school board, outright, with 53% of the vote! Over 8,000 people had voted for me. I was so shocked; I couldn't believe the win for days. I knew that the strategies we had implemented would be effective, but I never anticipated a landslide win.

This experience inspired me to share my own story, so that others can learn from the nascent tactics that we used and the incredible journey it took to get there.

Contents

Introduction

Welcome! If you've found yourself reading this book, it's likely because you are considering running for public office, are in the middle of your first campaign, or you are running for re-election during the COVID-19 pandemic (or, God forbid, a new one) and are looking for advice on what to do from someone who has been through it (that's me!)

Speaking from my own experiences in 2020, the old rules of campaigning got turned on its head when the pandemic hit the United States, three months after I announced my candidacy to become a trustee on the Washoe County School Board for District D.

In this book, I will share with you my own personal experience of being a first-time candidate running for election in the early stages of the pandemic, the tactics implemented to win (by 53% in the primary!) and used to help other candidates go on to win their elections afterward, despite the ongoing pandemic.

Lastly, near the end of the book, I will discuss what life was like being an elected official in 2021, and the disturbing events that led to my decision to resign from the school board for my health.

I'm including this rather dark part of my experience to give you a complete, very real, picture of my time in office. It is not to discourage you from beginning your own journey, instead it is intended to help you be better informed and equipped if you win a race, so that you enter public office and all that comes with your sworn duties, with eyes wide open and understand every potential outcome going into this. For me, I knew being in the spotlight would be hard but had no idea what the future held. I hope the stories in this book will both inspire you to run and harden your resolve in advance to be ready for anything.

If your heart is feeling full, I want you to know that I believe in you and I hope you find this book helpful and wish you the best of luck on the campaign trail!

Sincerely,
Kurt Thigpen

Chapter 1

Determine Your Why

Deciding to run for public office is truly one of the biggest, most vulnerable decisions you can ever make, and few choose to stick their necks out to go for it. It is not a choice you should make impulsively.

That's why, before you even consider announcing your candidacy or filing the paperwork, you need to sit down and do some deep introspection on *why* you want to run for public office.

What are the things you are most passionate about? What do you want to have an impact on? *Education, science, equal rights, curbing wasteful spending?*

What do *you* bring to the table that makes you unique and will it help you to serve your community?

For me, there were many reasons why I decided to run for the school board. The main issues I campaigned on were:

- Increase diversity, equity, and inclusion efforts in our schools so that all students and staff feel welcome to show up as their authentic selves.

- Improved transparency in between the board and the community. I realized many people didn't understand what was going on in their school communities until it was too late to voice their concerns, or even how the school district was different from the school board.

- Create a safer school environment for all students by increasing access to mental health services, working with local leaders to make pedestrian walkways safer for students, and updating crumbling infrastructure.

Those are just some of my "why's" for running. Now it's time for you to figure out yours depending on the office you're looking to run for.

Make a list to see if what you're passionate about falls within the jurisdiction of the office that you're hoping to be elected to. You may find a different public office is more suited to your list of "why's", and that's okay.

Above all, be honest with yourself, and take the time to do your homework about the elected role as well. Decide whether you can handle the duties, if elected, and what you will need to change in your life to make accommodations for a busier schedule.

Lastly, having a strong "why" behind your intent to run will help you with forming the foundation of your campaign.

If you don't have a list of strong believable

"why's" that resonate with a broad amount of voters, it's unlikely they'll feel encouraged to vote for you.

It all comes down to *why you?*.

Chapter 2

How to Start Your Campaign

So, you're ready to do this! Jumpstarting your campaign can feel like you're hitting the ground running. You go from nothing happening to everything happening very fast, and publicly, all at once!

Let's cover some of the overall things you'll need to do and think through, from prep-work to announcing your campaign publicly.

Decide Whether You Need Campaign Staff

Deciding whether or not you need, or can afford, a campaign staff is one of the first decisions you will need to make. It all depends on your free time, capabilities, and the average amount of funds one can typically raise for the office you're running for.

Common examples of campaign staff positions are campaign managers, fundraising managers, and field teams.

For my school board campaign, which is

commonly referred to as a "down-ballot campaign" (on the smaller side), I decided to hire two staff members. I settled on a campaign manager and a public relations person (my girl Rachel!) to make sure that I stay on message and can also help prepare me for media interviews, which I hadn't done much of in the past. As an introvert with ADHD, I thought this was a smart move!

If you cannot afford campaign staff, either for the entire election or at the beginning, there are many online resources that can help you like RunForSomething.org which puts out a TON of free information, resources, and some affordable courses you can take virtually to do things on your own, or with a small group of volunteers.

Prepare Your Friends & Family

One of the next, and most important steps, is sitting down with friends and family before you announce your intent to run for public office.

This may seem rather obvious, but this step covers many bases:

It gives them a heads up and time to process the news, so they aren't caught off guard.

You can instruct them on how to interact with the news media, should they reach out.

They can be on their best behavior (especially family.) Let's be honest, we've all seen candidates get dragged down because of a rogue family member or two.

Review Your Social Media Accounts

Unless you have lived off the grid your entire life, chances are you have some sort of digital footprint online that needs to be checked on before you make your announcement.

This isn't to say you have to come off as a "pure" candidate of choice, but it's best to do a little housekeeping so that voters see the best version of yourself instead of a more candid version.

Go through your social media accounts and make them private. Delete past posts that include profanity, days at the beach, awkward photos from high school - anything in a worst-case scenario that, if taken out of context, could be used against you in the campaign.

Some experts will recommend that you delete your personal social media accounts completely. I leave that up to you and your needs. For me, this wasn't an option as I am also a business owner and being active on social media is crucial to my work.

Just keep in mind that folks inside your bubble may not be as trustworthy as you think and could take screenshots of your private posts and send them to anyone. So, if you do end up keeping your personal accounts, even after making them private, I recommend doing what I like to call a "friend purge" and removing old high school friends you haven't talked to in 10 years, 2nd cousins you've never met, or that attractive person whose friend request you accepted but you've never actually spoken to or met in real life. Get rid of them and don't be sentimental.

Google Yourself

This always comes off as completely narcissistic, but it is going to be necessary for you to Google yourself before you announce your candidacy, during the campaign, and after, if you win, so you might as well start now.

Why is this important? So that you know what else is out there connected to you, aside from social media and can act upon it.

Examples of what you might find would be past articles you've written that may be reviewed and questioned your address information, or if you've lived an edgier past life, an arrest record!

Whatever may be out there, it's best to be aware of the search results so that you can create talking points ahead of time, should questions arise from the media or voters.

Keep Your Guard Up

Throughout the campaign, you will have a lot of different folks reach out to you through social media, email, text messages, phone calls, etc.

While it's good to engage with voters, you must set boundaries and be on guard as to how you choose to, or not to, answer certain questions.

Don't accept friend requests from people you have never met. Screen your phone calls, and if they leave a voicemail, call them back. Be careful about how you answer things in writing. Remember that anything you print can be used against you.

Create Your Campaign's Digital Presence

Once you've got your personal accounts handled, you can shift your attention to creating official, public campaign accounts for yourself.

This is highly recommended in the age of social media, as folks are going to want to look you up by name, and you want them to be directed to your public profiles rather than your personal (which feels intrusive.) These types of accounts are free to set up, and each social media platform has a "How To" section that you can use to get established.

At the very least, I would recommend you have a Facebook Page and a Twitter account as both are more conversational in nature, and you can easily monitor the buzz around the election, topics related to your race, and engage with the public.

Also, after you've filed, websites like Ballotpedia will automatically create a listing for all the candidates in your race. Be sure to claim your profile and update it with all of your campaign information, including a photo, as Ballotpedia is a highly trusted source for election information.

Lastly, you need to have a campaign website. I don't know how anyone running for office can win without one unless you're in a VERY small town.

I once had a friend, who I love, say that they just put their phone number out there for folks to just call them if they had questions about what they stood for.

This is not an ideal tactic, as folks are busy bees. If they can't find you online within a few seconds, they will be less likely to give you their vote.

Having a website also helps you rank higher on sites like Google and Bing when voters search for your name, and you want them to go to the right place, *your place*, to learn about your "why's" for running for office.

If your campaign has a small budget and you're worried about cost, you can buy domain names pretty cheaply at providers like BlueHost.com, and they usually have great bundles for first-time accounts for the first year. You'll likely spend less than $100 if you host with them and use their site builder, but if you can afford to hire a professional, that would be my preference. You want to put your best foot forward, right?

Learn Your Local, State, or Federal Campaign Rules & Laws

It may surprise you to learn that there are rules at every level for political campaigns from how your signage must read, to the appropriate way and time you need to submit donation information.

This varies depending on the type of office you are seeking, as well as the geographic area you live in. There could be city, county, and state laws (sometimes referred to as "Codes of Ethics") that you have to be aware of. If you are found to be in violation of one of these ordinances, you could face a small fine, or worse, receive negative media attention around a faux pas.

Do some research online or consult someone within election offices at your local government to find out what you should know when it comes to filing for your candidacy, registering as a political committee to accept donations, when your financial filing deadlines are due, and anything else you may need to know.

When I went to file my candidate paperwork at the county office, they had a nifty little packet for me that had all of this information, and my campaign manager helped me keep an eye on these things so that I didn't have to.

Chapter 3

Fundraising Compassionately During a Pandemic

Every campaign must raise money to have a chance at succeeding. Print materials, advertising, staff, etc., all cost money and it's not easy to fundraise, especially if you haven't done it before in some capacity.

I'll be honest with you - it is **extremely** awkward to ask people you know for money, let alone strangers. But this is ten times harder when we're in the middle of a pandemic that is causing all kinds of economic hardship and uncertainties.

I grappled with how to do this, if at all, during my campaign.

When the first lockdown was implemented, I had only raised about $2500 for the campaign, and this was due in large part to three private fundraisers I was able to hold beforehand.

Little did I know, I wouldn't host any more in-person fundraisers for the rest of the campaign. This was mostly due to lengthy restrictions on public gatherings, as well as how taboo we all felt at that time about leaving our homes just to go to the grocery store, even with masks on.

Some candidates, that I knew, had decided to pause fundraising indefinitely, while others were more discrete and sensitive in how they went about it. My campaign manager, Adam, was adamant that we increase call time asking for donations rather than pausing everything completely (it was his job, after all, to push the envelope.) After placing a few calls to some business owners, it was very obvious that it wasn't the time - they were all worried about making payroll, keeping the doors open, and putting food on the table. They were not concerned with the election that was still three months away.

So, I decided to give it some time, and instead focused on helping the community (more on this in chapter six.)

I can't tell you exactly when it was that it felt right to start asking for funds again, but I just had a gut feeling about the timing, probably a few weeks later, and some ideas came to fruition on how to ask less intrusively.

We had to get creative, and be sensitive and intentional, about moving forward.

Collect Donations Safely and Easily Online

First, we installed an affordable, easy-to-use non-partisan online donation tool (we used <u>DonorBox.org</u>) on the website so people could easily give as little, or as much as they could - since we couldn't do big in-person parties anymore.

I recommend a non-partisan tool so that you don't turn off folks from different political parties. Remember, you're running to serve the people, not a party (I would hope.)

Then, we peppered "small asks" into our social media and email communications with campaign supporters.

For example, I created a social media post that said: "For $20, or a month's worth of Starbucks visits, you can become a recurring donor to support our campaign. You won't miss it!"

We received two monthly recurring donors after that, and several one-time donations because it made people think *"what the heck, it's just $20, right?"* It is an easy amount to part with.

At the end of my campaign, the average donation was calculated to be roughly $25 per person, so I think the "small asks" were effective, and a little fun!

My favorite small ask was when I had drawn a caricature on a thank you card to a donor I knew and posted a picture of it on social media saying, "If you would like a custom doodle on your thank you card by yours truly, chip in $20 today!".

It worked! I knew that folks would appreciate receiving something personal from me. I felt so clever!

Take Advantage of New Developments

It's basic psychology that it is very easy to play off of folks' frustrations and anger and, frankly, school boards, in general, are easy targets. So, anytime something would occur that I was vehemently against, I would inform my supporters and vow to do something about it once elected.

For example, you could say something along the lines of: "I'm just as frustrated as you all are about last night's school board vote, and I hope to do something about it if elected. But, to get there, I need your support to reach as many voters as possible since we can't knock on doors. Chip in what you can on our website."

Sometimes I would speak to goals or costs of campaign materials we needed and always made it time sensitive. The sense of urgency combined with public frustration was a useful tactic.

Know Your Audience Before Asking

We would never call a random list of strangers asking for money. They don't know you, so why would they give you a penny?

Start by calling friends and family, tell them how excited you are and how you could use their support if they're able to chip in. Keep these types of asks informal, so that they don't feel like your relationship would be damaged if they declined.

I usually lead with "I'm trying to get between $50-$100 per call right now if you're able to help." Sometimes it worked, and they'd either handle it on the phone, or other times they'd wait for a bit, and I'd receive a surprise check in the mail.

If they're hesitant, don't forget to mention how easy it is to make a donation on your campaign website and to tell them the address. Make them write it down by asking if they have a pen and paper ready, as that will make it more likely that they'll remember to do it.

Aside from friends and family, you need a relevant audience, because without being able to hitch your ask to something that connects you and the caller, you're wasting your time.

Here are a Few More Fundraising Tactics That Were Useful:

- Get a list of donors from other campaigns similar to yours, or at different levels, as it's all public record, and ethical to do so. Write a relevant letter to each group about how it's clear your values align because of X, and they should donate because of

Y. I was endorsed by my predecessor on the school board, and she gave me her list of donors. I sent a mailer to folks saying, "with their endorsement, I am also asking for your support in my campaign".

- If you're part of a political party, request a contact list to send either an email or letter to past party donors or registered members.

- Now that vaccines are available, depending on your city/state COVID safety mandates, you could host small fundraisers hosted by influential folks you know, and invite a select group of people with a history of large campaign donations. This is a gamble, mind you, as we're still in the pandemic so, be sure that if you do proceed, that you do so following all the rules, and perhaps going beyond them by requiring proof of vaccination or something like that.

Chapter 4

How to Reach Voters Safely & Strategically

What to Do When You Can't Go Door-Knocking

One of the first things Adam and I tried to establish was how on earth could we reach voters if we couldn't knock on doors, shake hands and kiss proverbial babies the traditional way?

Before the lockdown, we had *just* printed up 2000 walk cards to use to go knock on doors with.

Sadly, the majority of them ended up getting recycled because, at the early point in the pandemic, it felt *incredibly* inappropriate to invade folks' personal bubbles during a period of lockdown, even just to leave some information on their doorstep.

The last thing I wanted in the news was a headline that said, "School Board Candidate Ignores Lockdown with Door Knocking." Not a good look.

We ended up including the door walking material

in with donor mailers to make folks feel a bit more special, along with my candidate business card. This also made the mailers feel thick and heavy, which does something psychologically to us to make us feel like we just received something really important, and we must open it.

The lesson learned here is: **Always go for the printable door-to-door walk cards that can hook on doorknobs**, as I don't think door-knocking will be making a quick return until the pandemic is in the rearview mirror, and we also never know when/if one will come again! Let's not waste paper.

Pro Tip: You can punch a hole in the corner of the walk card and put a rubber band through it to hang it on doors. This also prevents the wind from littering the ground with them. I wish I had thought of this. Be sure to wear gloves and a face-covering if you do go out and about! Safety first.

On the Subject of Yard Signs

I didn't have *one* yard sign for my campaign. They are very expensive and, to me, only serve one's ego.

Not to mention, there were fewer people on the road than normal at the height of the pandemic so, who was going to see them?!

Instead, we found a creative and fun alternative.

Since we did have requests for yard signs,

some very insistent ones too (be ready), it was still considered bad form to go to people's houses for any reason, my campaign created printable signs you could download from our website, print out at home, and tape up in your window if you so desired.

I don't know how many people actually did this, but it was there for folks who asked, and I choose to tell myself that they were everywhere, just not on any of my regular routes around town, haha.

Create a Communications Outreach Plan

As a digital marketer, it was obvious that we would have to use a variety of tools to reach many voters through different mediums, so I crafted a communication plan to get in front of as many voters in my district as possible, from all demographics.

Here are Some Tactics We Recommend Using:

- Social media promotion was easy enough to keep going. Consistent, engaging, and helpful posts, including live streams and videos with experts on different topics important to the community (such as ways of dealing with stress during isolation), would go a long way. Also, create a private Facebook Group for supporters to stay informed on how they can help, and create fun graphics for folks to use as a Facebook Profile Frame with your campaign logo on it!

- Invest in social media advertising. It's still relatively cheap to place ads on all social media platforms, quick to set up, and you're usually able to target only the folks that live in your area who can vote for you and weed out the folks that can't, which is important, so that you don't waste your money.

- Say "yes!" to any and all chances at news interviews, being on virtual panel discussions, writing opinion pieces for local newspapers, radio interviews, and consider paying for an online advertorial or your own dedicated radio spot if you can afford it. I actually went on the radio several times after being invited and eventually paid for some half-hour spots in which I got to talk about the issues that mattered most to me.

This got me in front of a completely different demographic than I was used to. I focused on discussing the issues most can agree with and not on the politics of the day. This is where my public relations staff, Rachel "Save the Day" Gattuso would pull me aside or call me ahead of time to keep me centered and on message, reminding me to be myself at the end of the day so the voters could get to know me.

Google Advertising & Search Engine Optimization

If your state allows for it, place Google Search ads for anyone searching for your name, as well as your opponents' names, to ensure that your website comes up every time, and prominently.

Name recognition is crucial in elections, and especially vital during the pandemic, when I knew that mail-in ballots would be used and folks would be at home searching candidate races they were unaware of.

So, it's very important that voters can easily find you first in an online search.

This is also why your website needs to be keyword optimized for search engines (Search Engine Optimization) as well so that you can rank high on Google organically (without ads) when people search for you or something relevant to your race.

Other Grassroots Tactics

- Pay for a subscription to a voter information system, often through a political party, to get information on voters in your district (mailing address, phone numbers, political affiliation, etc.,) so that you and volunteers can set up a remote phone banking operation.

- Don't underestimate the power of direct mail. I went a conservative route with it and only paid to send two on my own campaign's dime to target non-partisans and others in my district. I also knew when sample ballots would be sent to households and timed it so that the first postcard mailer got sent to voters that same day, and the second, larger piece, a couple a week or so before mail-in ballots were first sent out.

Chapter 5

Get Those Endorsements

Unless you're already famous, getting thousands of people to know your name in a short amount of time, through remote means of outreach, is a challenging prospect.

And what are they going to think when you're still a nobody to them?

This is why I focused on boosting my campaign's image by seeking a large number of endorsements from community leaders, spiritual leaders, unions, and close friends who were highly regarded in the community or had impressive titles after their names.

I suppose you would call that influencer marketing, but I refuse (ha!) This grassroots tactic worked well as we would post one or two endorsements a week, and the more we did, the more I would hear from others "I see you everywhere on Facebook," or "do you have to be someone special to endorse you?" to which I would reply, "no! The more the merrier."

Aside from social media, we would list each

endorsement as a special announcement on the website's news section. For the larger endorsements, from unions and national organizations, we put their logos on the homepage of the website, front, and center.

A little legitimacy goes a long way, I think.

If voters see you have the most backing, psychologically they want to back the winning horse. So, endorsements give you that leverage.

How Do You Get Larger Endorsements?

It's easy enough to get people you know to endorse you. It's complicated to know where to begin with larger endorsements like labor unions and national organizations that are politically active.

My experience was that these entities will, 90% of the time, reach out to all the candidates directly for a chance at a panel interview to choose which candidate, if any, they will want to back. When this happens, be sure to do your homework on the organization and matters important to them.

Other national organizations such as Run for Something, the LGBTQ+ Victory Fund, and Moms for Office, as some examples, have applications on their websites you have to fill out, and sometimes an *extensive* approval process, so get those applications in early!

Chapter 6

Help Your Community

Something that should matter to anyone running for public office is the community you hope to serve.

At the height of the pandemic, many folks were struggling with shortages of face masks, hand sanitizer, toilet paper, and more, if you recall.

When we paused our fundraising efforts, and even after the campaign was over, my team of volunteers would keep track of needs within the community, particularly those of the school district since I was running for a seat on the school board.

I had many friends, who worked in all areas of the school district, that I reached out to and asked how I could use my platforms to help. I'm so delighted when I think back at the many ways, we were able to do this, that I wish I could do it all again as it brings my heart so much joy.

Here are Some of the Ways We Did Our Part:

One campaign volunteer made cloth face masks

with her daughter, and I was able to source some from her to deliver to folks who couldn't find masks.

A client of mine happened to have 600 extra face shields on hand that I was able to negotiate to be donated to the school district, and I delivered them myself to spread some cheer, along with doughnuts for the staff who had been working so hard on getting PPE ready for schools to reopen.

We created a Mutual Aid Resources page on the campaign website to make sure folks knew where they could get essentials like food. They could also connect with online groups full of people looking to help one another however they could.

We did winter clothing drives for children who couldn't afford to buy a coat after their parents were laid off due to the pandemic.

We were even able to do a fundraiser and khaki pants drive for one school that had many kids coming back that couldn't afford new clothes. We raised over $1500 and filled up my SUV with bags and bags of khakis pants of all sizes. They had enough funds left over to buy winter rain jackets for the kids!

Lastly, and probably my favorite occasion, was when I learned of one child whose family was hit so hard economically that they couldn't afford to pay for the debt accrued on their school lunch bill (this was before the Dept. of Agriculture released funds for free lunches to all students during the pandemic.) I think the family didn't want to apply for food assistance, as it can make many feel ashamed (I've been there before, when I was a kid.)

It gave me great joy to show up at the school and make a donation to wipe that student's debt clean, as I firmly believe no child should ever go to school hungry. They never knew it was me, and I haven't really told too many people about that until now, because to me it was always about my *why*, and being there for the students was one of them.

Some experiences we shared on social media to make folks aware of certain needs, and some we kept to ourselves as it's the simple act of giving back to the community that was important to me, especially if we have the ability to do so.

I still do this today, even after my short time on the school board (we'll dive into that in Chapter seven.)

The world could use more random acts of kindness from those who care and want to be helpful.

After the long, stressful year that was 2021, we could all use a bit more kindness, grace, patience, and a sense of community spirit.

We're all in this together, whether we realize it or not.

Chapter 7

Winning & the Reality of Public Service

Picture it, if you can. You did it! You actually won your election.

I want you to be in, and stay in, this mindset with me so that I can prepare you for the time between being elected and actually getting sworn in (in my case I had to wait 6 **whole** months as trustee-elect), as well as the time being in the hot seat and things I learned that you should do or avoid like the plague (pun intended.)

Election Day is Surreal

It was June 9th, 2020, the date of the primary election.

I was up against two opponents, one of whom ended up becoming my friend, and the other I don't have much to say about because we never really met (due to the pandemic and because we only saw each other on Zoom panel interviews.)

It was such an odd day. I was nervous, jumpy, and just didn't want to be in the house. So, my husband and I did our own staycation at a luxury suite at one of the resorts in Reno to try and relax and to take time to rest. I tried to focus on the fact that, no matter the results, I knew that I ran a very compassionate, caring, and student-focused campaign.

I left it all on the field. Now it was up to the voters.

Little did I know, this day would end up being one of the largest voter turnouts in Nevada history. Many folks chose to show up in person, waiting in line for hours at polling stations to cast their vote, and others played it safe due to COVID, by mailing their ballots in (I did! Never going back to the machine again.)

I would watch the local news, which I never do, and felt like I was watching paint dry so, I would alternate between reading, watching movies, or talking to family. I still had my phone in my hand, no matter what I did, constantly refreshing 3 different election result websites to see if one had the scoop before the other.

Adam was there (he brought pizza and bubbly) and we had planned on watching the results live on TV like in the "before times," but as the hours went on, and several phone calls from connections who acted as the boots on the ground, we learned that we weren't going to be hearing any announcements from the Secretary of State's office that night. Bummer.

So, we called it a night, and everyone but Chris (my husband) and I got in bed with our cozy hotel robes and watched a movie until we fell asleep.

I usually have trouble sleeping. I've battled with insomnia on and off for years, but oddly enough I knocked out pretty easily. Perhaps my body was ready to release **all** the energy and tension from campaigning.

However, for no reason at all, I sat up and looked at the time. It was 3:05 am. I wasn't sure if poll workers, or anybody out there was working around the clock, but used my thumb to spin that refresh page wheel on my iPhone and low and behold: **I won**.

Not only did I win, but it was a landslide victory!

53% of the people who voted in my district believed in me and remembered my name. They believed in the passionate messages we put out there. They had just elected the first openly gay school board trustee on record in Washoe County, and possibly even the State itself (it is really hard to verify these things, let me tell you.)

I felt so many things at once; an immediate sense of duty, disbelief, joy, shock, fear, and wondering if this is real life, or are we really living in the Matrix (hey, we all do it) or if Ashton Kutcher had brought his show Punk'D back **just** for this moment.

I pinched myself. Nope, this was real life, folks.

What you have to understand is that the most astonishing thing wasn't the fact that I won (I was confident I'd at least make it through the primary, with all the work we did,) but the chess-like way that I had won.

Checkmate! Folks, the biggest factor of all was the percentage.

You see, Nevada law states that if a candidate in a county race wins in the primary election with **50% of the vote plus 1 other person** (wild, right? I want to meet that *one* person if this ever gets that close) then that candidate wins not just the election, but the seat itself, outright, and does not have a General Election in November.

Pretty sure my mouth dropped when it dawned on me that I was done. I didn't have to stress or campaign anymore.

I marveled for a while thinking about the 6-month marathon remote marketing campaign. We weren't sure it would work, but because of the pandemic, I think it allowed us to reach **more** people than we could have door-knocking.

I felt so good for weeks after. I was the Trustee-Elect for the Washoe County School Board, District D - loud and proud!

What happens next? I wondered.

It was time to put on pants, that much I knew.

I looked at my vibrating phone, saw a number I didn't know and knew things were about to get interesting! It was a reporter.

Interacting with Reporters

One of the first things that happens to you, after you win an election, (aside from the barrage of congratulations & good wishes from friends, family & the community,) were calls, texts, and emails from reporters across the state, some even out of state, wanting me to comment on the outcome.

I knew I needed to talk to Adam and Rachel - assemble the team! This is why having support is so important, it was especially helpful to have Rachel's PR prowess and Adam's knowledge of whether the numbers typically change or stay the same. Mail-in ballots were still being counted and would be for

37

weeks after election day.

My team helped to keep me calm and informed. They helped me decide if I wanted to respond to the media requests and what the message was going to be.

I felt good after putting our heads together, and I remember taking a call from The Nevada Independent and the reporter asking how I felt, and if I had planned on claiming victory at that moment.

I'm a very cautious person, so my intuition (and my own self-doubt) decided that we wouldn't be claiming anything at that moment since ballots were still being counted, and that we of course feel so thankful for everyone's support and that my team would be keeping an eye on the numbers, and it was time for me to go rest.

Good job, Trustee-Elect.

I pretty much said the same thing that day to any reporter that reached out to me. As the day got longer and the points got higher, Adam got me fired up that "statistically, there is no way this is going to change." In my giddiness, I couldn't help myself. I sent out a tweet thanking everyone for their support, for helping me get elected, and that I had a lot of work to do to get ready for the position come January 2021.

Luckily, the numbers stayed the same and I didn't end up with egg on my face, ha! But the point is, you should always be prepared when talking to the media, especially when you are in your feelings at that moment and must stay consistent with your messaging until you're ready to make your move.

It was important to me that whenever I was ready, I would use my own voice, not someone else's or a publication's, to declare victory. I wanted it in writing, coming from my accounts, so that word for word, my future constituents knew I was speaking from the heart. It is also way less stressful if you don't have to worry about being misquoted. I highly recommend owning your voice and using it at the right times.

The last thing I'll say about reporters is that you need to always remember, they need *you* more than you need *them*. Because without you, there is a missing component to their story. Always know you can decline to provide comments and interviews.

Okay, actually, there is one more piece of advice on this subject- **always** be clear whether you are speaking with reporters on or off the record. I've been burned before by someone saying things like "oh, now it's just me and you talking," to get me to let my guard down, only to find my quotes in a future story.

I've learned that you need to **firmly** ask, "are we (or can we) speaking off the record?" and you must get an affirmative answer from that reporter before you open your mouth again.

Always be cautious and remember that they're just doing their job!

Chapter 8

Preparing for Office & Becoming a Public Figure

Let's face it, going from private life to being held accountable to the public, seemingly overnight, is a tough pill to swallow. It doesn't matter how large or small the elected position is, it has a heft to it. That's why I was thankful that I had time to mentally prepare for this new dynamic, as I'm actually a very introverted person.

Your name will be mentioned in the news all the time, for good, bad, and mostly neutral reasons as **sometimes** it's just the news! You'll hear folks mention that they saw you on TV, stop you at an event to see if it's really you, or a relative who watched the meeting you were at. You will have to adjust to the weird feeling that you are being spoken to more formally than before, and your name is preceded by your elected designation. I never got used to being greeted as "Trustee Thigpen" when on school grounds, but it does make you feel honored and humbled.

As you're now going to be in the public eye, I highly recommend setting boundaries for yourself, your family, the general public, and your own environment.

For me, that meant I had to resist Googling myself, reading articles with my face on them, and avoiding being on social media comment sections (as that is literally the 5th Circle of Hell.)

When Do You Start and How to Take Advantage of the Time

Depending on the rules that govern elections where you live, after you win an election, some folks are immediately sworn in the next day, or soon after, and other institutions run on different calendars.

For the school board, I had to wait to be sworn into office on January 4th, 2021. So, I had an entire six months to get ready.

Honestly, this was a godsend as I got to spend so much time getting to know the administration, reading every recommended book, studying recent decisions related to education in the legislature, and much more. Superintendent Dr. Kristen McNeill even reached out to me privately to congratulate me and said, "this is my cell, and you feel free to call me anytime if you have questions." This was helpful because, of course, I had **a lot** of questions and requested her input as the months slowly ticked by.

I still consider her a friend and look up to her to

this day. I'll never forget the dedication she put into keeping schools and teaching going, in what has to be the hardest time in our modern history.

Those months, before taking on the mantle, made me feel like I was stuck in limbo. I was ready and waiting anxiously because I like to be helpful. But you have to learn to walk before you can run, so absorb as much information as you can from the outside before you're officially on the inside.

This strategy really helped me a lot later in monitoring not just my actions but also in understanding my colleagues on the board, and how processes and procedures worked (oftentimes slowly and frustratingly, in my opinion) on a board like this.

Staying Out of Trouble & Maintaining Balance

One of the most important things to brush up on ahead of time is your area's Open Meeting Laws and other policies that oversee your specific role, or governing entity, that you may have been elected to serve.

If you violate certain laws during a meeting, for example, or while texting colleagues you serve with, you could be looking at paying some serious fines, negative press, and in the worst-case scenario, a request for you to resign. Be careful what you put in writing as your communications are now considered part of the public record that can be requested unless you're speaking with legal counsel.

For the school board, we had **thick** binders full of board policies, state statutes, and legal documents that I needed to familiarize myself so as not to put a foot wrong on day one. I'm glad I started reading before starting the job because there will always be more reading to do!

The school board had also adopted a very progressive Balanced Governance Model based on the principles written by my friend Dr. Thomas Alsbury, who is one of the most patient and kind people I've ever met. I read his book, on improving school board effectiveness while in the limbo state, and it really helped shape my mindset on how to work as a team. I learned how to be able to disagree respectfully, not to tear one another apart or make things political, and also to try and avoid taking a firm position on something, so that your colleagues won't feel like they can't negotiate with you or that you've backed them in a corner.

I took this to heart once in the seat, as often constituents and supporters would want to know what I thought about an agenda item before a board meeting, and my answer was usually the same: "I know how I will feel after I see the staff's presentation." Nobody likes to hear that, but it did keep me out of pre-committing myself to a decision that I may end up changing my mind about after listening to the staff and my peers. I try to keep that in mind with everything. Wait for the facts, talk things through, make the best decision you can.

I find that the Balanced Governance Model can be applied to almost anything in life, professionally, and in public office where you have to work in a group setting to accomplish something, but the model only works when **everyone** adopts the model, and unfortunately that doesn't always happen, which really frustrated and disappointed me at times as seeing someone go rogue to please their political base did nothing to improve the lives of students.

But you have to remember that in public office, as it is in life, you are only responsible for your actions and only you can control your reaction to events. Ignore the partisan distractions and grandstanding and just focus on showing up to work; be prepared and ready to go.

This might sound idealistic, and, in some ways, it is. It can be hard and may eventually weigh you down. We're all human after all.

Try not to take any bait from others and try and ignore any other distractions created by someone you might end up serving with or are part of the same elected body or the actions of their supporters. I can tell you from experience, worrying about that is a long, dark, unending road.

Pro Tip: Always remember that **no** decision you make in office will make **everyone** happy, and people usually only reach out when they're angry about something. In almost all decisions I had a hand in making, it always felt like 50% of folks were delighted and the other 50% was vowing to recall you for voting the way you did! Sometimes making the tough calls means making no one happy, including yourself. Being a school board member during a pandemic means having to make stressful decisions around whether or not it's safe to allow more kids to come back for in-person learning vs. staying on distance learning, if students should be required to wear masks outside at recess, and more. Who knew school boards would find themselves in these decisions and the division around them?

So, as best as you can, develop a "thick skin" and be ready for unfair and crude emails and in-person public comments. Try to remember that most folks are busy living their lives, can't keep up with every meeting or matter, and that's why the voters elected *you* to be in the seat and to sort things out for them. They picked you for a reason, right?

Chapter 9

End of the Road for Me, But Hope for the Future

I can't tell you how honored I was that people believed in me enough to vote me into office. I grew up as a trailer park kid in rural Georgia that eventually came out west for a chance at a better life. I did it and I love the life I built for myself.

But the more I did for my community over time, and saw the impacts that I could make, I realized that I was really good at leading and finding creative solutions. It sparked a dream that I always had to run for office, and for some reason before I turned 30.

I achieved that goal on June 9, 2020, when I was 29 when elected and on Jan. 4, 2021, I was 30 (I'm a Cancer for those wondering.)

Despite all obstacles, I was able to realize a dream I had as a little boy.

I've certainly come a long way, but sometimes the path forward has very sharp turns, and it had many for me during my time as a school board trustee.

I entered into office at a time when the nation was, and still is, deeply divided. Two days after my inauguration, the January 6th Insurrection took place at the U.S. Capitol, and the school district took notice of organized activity from hate groups, and each school board was getting filled with people (some of whom didn't live in the school district, or have kids in it) spreading misinformation about diversity and equity measures, sex-ed, anti-LGBTQ+ sentiments, and more popularly (as we've seen across the country,) anger over school closures, that masks are required to be worn by all students, and at the possibility that we would require vaccinations of all children, even though that was in the health district's purview, not ours.

Photo credit: Jason Bean, Reno-Gazette Journal

I remember at my first board meeting; we had a huge school police presence after the Insurrection. Our concern was, if something like that can happen at the heart of the U.S. government, who is to say that we won't be next, especially with the fervor we were hearing from some groups. The school police were there to protect us, and members of the public, and they stayed for every meeting after that, as the threat level increased.

Across the country we were seeing board rooms getting stormed, school board members getting screamed at, harassed, beaten, and doxed. The situation was, and still is, worrying. Here in Washoe County, things continued to get worse leading up to every meeting.

I received endless hate mail around my sexuality, that I was trying to impose my "gay agenda" on students by approving a Brave Space program where students can go to feel welcome and safe, no matter their identity or background. Some individuals would declare they would remove us from our seats "one way or another" or recall us if we didn't vote a certain way.

It came to a head when these groups, all at the same time as though it were planned, tried to storm the auditorium we were meeting in. Staff had to put themselves in harm's way to stop them. I'm told that one of the assailants told a school police officer that he better choose a side now because "it's coming."

In that same meeting, I was informed that there were also lone individuals who broke off from the main group and were trying to gain access to the stage where we were seated for our meeting.

Understandably, I started fearing for my safety, especially being openly LGBTQ+ and being very aware of the increased rate of violence on members of our community. Folks would come to meetings specifically to condemn my very existence, with LGBTQ+ children in the room and likely watching online. I can't justify those actions.

One of the worst parts was when someone doxed me and my colleagues, members of the school board and the superintendent, online (sharing our private phone numbers and home addresses) and rallied folks to "drag them out of their homes."

I felt like a sitting duck after this. We installed security measures at home and at my office. The school police chief sent me information on evasive maneuvers and how to be mindful of my surroundings. I felt as though an attack of some sort was imminent, after seeing similar activity across the country.

I've written publicly about this part, and have been open about the level of stress, pressure, fear, and paranoia that took on my mental and physical health.

I was just a person, living in a community, who saw an opportunity to be able to help make a difference in children's lives. Suddenly, I was an enemy that others had their sights on, hell-bent to get rid of "by any means necessary."

I kept telling myself that my skin just wasn't thick enough yet. It wasn't until I began to have more chronic insomnia, panic attacks, and my body felt like it was falling apart, that a doctor told me the job was literally killing me with the amount of stress I was experiencing. Things were so bad that I battled every day with suicidal ideations that I hadn't felt since I was a teenager.

I explained to my doctor what had been going on and, mouth aghast, the doctor told me, point-blank, what I was exposing myself to was recurring trauma. At that time, I don't think I could see the forest for the trees, so it was a bit of a wake-up call.

It wasn't until a friend, and teacher who was one of the few I could confide in said to me, "you know, you can always resign if things are getting worse. We will still love and support you."

It was the permission and validation I needed. So, in May, just five months into a four-year term, I decided to resign citing medical reasons. I stayed on until July to help fill another empty seat on the board, but I attended all but my last board meeting virtually. When I was physically in that room it would trigger a panic attack strong enough to make me sweat through my clothing and cause my face to twitch uncontrollably under my face mask.

I stayed quiet on the specifics around my

departure as I was just focused on finishing up and letting the board appoint someone to take my place, after I officially resigned in July.

It ate at me that my big win, the good work others had done to get me there, felt as if it had gone to waste. Someone on Facebook said I was a "waste of a vote". I felt that it was important to let the constituents know the truth about the dangers, hateful rhetoric, threats, and harassment we had to sit through. I wrote about how much it had taken from my mental and physical health, and mentioned the suicidal thoughts, and that I knew I was no good serving anyone if I wasn't taking care of myself.

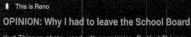

❚ This is Reno

OPINION: Why I had to leave the School Board

Kurt Thigpen photo, used with permission. By Kurt Thigpen. I have debated since late May when my impending resignation was...

Jul 28, 2021

I put all of my truth into an opinion piece for ThisIsReno.com that went viral locally, and blew up internationally, a month after it was posted because of my openness about my mental health struggles and my plea for civility. Suddenly CBS was calling me for an interview, and publications like Newsweek, Yahoo.com, the Associated Press, NPR, and ProPublica were amplifying my experience to endless localities.

I didn't expect my words to go **that** far. For me, the article's purpose was to act as a form of closure, letting the community know what was going on, and for them to step up, and to encourage others who are suffering from mental health crises during this pandemic to feel that it's okay to talk about our struggles openly, and to seek help. I wanted to throw a giant hammer to shatter the stigma around mental health and bring awareness that, if a high-ranking elected official like me can suffer and find a way to make it through the darkness, so can they.

Now, I'm doing much better after taking the time to lay low, recharge, work on healing, and receive regular mental health treatment that I had never had access to before. I was surprised by a diagnosis of ADHD and PTSD. I'm still learning, and I am a work in progress, like anyone else. I remain resilient and the fire that led me to run for office is still there. I often feel like I'm not doing enough, and want to go full throttle again, but 2021 taught me to be a bit more gentle with myself if I want to be here in the long run.

I don't feel that I **need** to run for office again, at least not anytime soon. But I have been asked to help others running for office and have helped some really good people get elected from behind the scenes from judges to regents, city council members, and more. They saw the fire in me and helped me realize that I can combine my passions in different ways. I can utilize the platform I now have, combined with my sense of duty, and I might be able to make a bigger difference to many people all over the world who, too, want to do their part to make the world a better place.

That is why I wrote this book detailing how an introverted, openly gay Millennial with mental health issues, no children, and who came from a poor background, was able to defy the odds and win an election by historic margins, before the age of 30.

If I can do it, you can too. We need more people with that fire running for office. Now you have the advantage of obtaining the knowledge of how to pull it off from someone who did it, despite the pandemic, and other obstacles that ended up in our way. You'll find the right path to overcome anything.

I have decided that my purpose in life now, and what has always made me truly happy, is to work to create a positive social impact based on sharing my own experiences. Whether those experiences are inspiring or act as a cautionary tale, I hope they have helped at least one of you keep the flame going. I hope they help you understand the weight of public office as you consider your options in running for election or not.

I want you to keep in mind that what happened to me was unique and that me sharing my truth isn't meant to scare you off. It's to equip you with more tools and knowledge so that you, and others, can be the change we need in the world. When you are in service to your community, and with each person rising up and working together to heal our divisions, I know we can turn things around.

It is my sincere hope that by being open and vulnerable with you about my own journey, good and bad, and by providing the "secrets" behind my own electoral success and others I've helped, you will be able to use the same processes to go forth and change the world - for the better.

You've got this. I believe in you. Know that if you feel passionate enough about helping a cause in your community, big or small, that fire alone qualifies you to run for office.

Don't let the norms of the past tell you any differently.

Together we will keep proving them wrong.

Epilogue

Thank you for making it this far in the book, and I hope that sharing my own experiences, from campaigning during a pandemic and the things I've learned, can help those of you who are brave enough to answer the call of service during this time. I hope that this book will continue to be useful in the future, as there will always be new challenges to face.

In my opinion, running for office from a stance of servant leadership will never fail you, no matter how much divisiveness you end up witnessing in politics, or the games that are played.

What is most important is to focus on your *why* and the people whose lives you are trying to make better in some way. It is important to take care of not just the community you live in, but yourself as well.

For whoever ends up reading this, no matter who you are, your background, your religion, nationality, gender identity or expression, sexuality, or the color of your skin - know that in America, you belong, and if you hear that call to service, you are more than worthy to answer the call.

Good luck to you all, and I wish you wisdom, safety, humility, and strength for whatever journey lies ahead for you.

Yours sincerely,
Kurt Thigpen

About the Author

 **Kurt Thigpen** is a former Trustee for the Washoe County School Board in Nevada, a writer, CEO of Ace Studios, a social impact marketing agency, and an openly gay mental health advocate, especially after being diagnosed with adult ADHD and PTSD.

He was born and raised in rural Hazlehurst, Georgia, and moved to Reno, Nevada in 2011 after graduating from Southeastern Technical College with an Associate's Degree in Web Design.

Since moving to Reno, he has served on multiple non-profit boards, membership associations, mentored young LGBTQ+ people, and given talks around the country about the need for more diversity, equity, and inclusion in advertising and the workforce.

Kurt is a firm believer in giving back to one's community once you've become successful in life and works to lift others up any chance he gets. His leadership style stems from a deep sense of empathy towards others after many challenges in his own life.

He is married to actor, writer, artist, and comedian Chris Thigpen since 2015 and they live very happily together with their two dogs, Finn and Flo, and their cat Fiona.

You can keep in touch by visiting his website at www.kurtthigpen.com.

Made in the USA
Las Vegas, NV
02 February 2022

42887828R00039